More Life

More Life

EMBRACE THE CHALLENGE OF LIFE!

Joe Brazzle

ISBN: 1979801223
ISBN 13: 9781979801225

This book is dedicated to the ray of sunshine that found me hiding in the darkness. Thank you, Rhea Jasmine, for your brutal honesty and never-ending love!

May the road be gentle on your feet.
May the wind be in your favor.
May the sun always shine upon your face.
And may you see God in everything that you do!
Godspeed.

Contents

Foreword

About five years ago, Joe told me he was on to something. He was running retreats for wounded warriors and he told me he was one step closer to figuring out the best way to aid others in becoming self-reliant, adventurous, and productive members of society. How to teach people to make the best hand out of whatever cards they were dealt. How to help others learn from his mistakes, attempts, and successes. I still have the index card that I wrote his simple wisdom on; it reads:

1. *I am my own resource.*
2. *If I say yes, the possibilities are endless.*
3. *Think and act only about the things that serve you well.*

Over the years, Joe turned these humble mantras into a holistic philosophy that describes how anyone—a wounded warrior, a deadbeat dad, a single mother, a child, a regular guy, a successful entrepreneur, anyone—can become the best version of himself or herself.

I recently started the practice of writing and reciting affirmations for myself. I previously thought that I could read a book with a good idea in it, and I would somehow benefit from merely reading it. Since I started writing down my affirmations (often derived from lessons I got from books just like this one) and reciting them to myself each morning, however, I realized that reading is only the first step. To make the good advice stick, you need to believe it, remind yourself of it, and determine the daily actions that will make it benefit your real life. Daily affirmations and turning wishes into actions happen to be two tricks I learned from Joe over the years. I sincerely hope you take as much out of his book as I have from my longtime friendship with him. I hope you adopt the right mind-sets and make the right choices to make the most out of the one life you were given.

Start with a quick read through this book. As you go, answer the journaling questions honestly and briefly. Then dwell on the "Actions On" sections. Read through a few of the referenced books and talk about what you've learned with your friends and family. Then in a month from now, read this book again. Look at your old journal entries. Update them. Are you on the right track? What's working for you? What isn't?

One thing I've learned over and over from Joe is that even though I am my own best resource, if I really want to be successful I need to talk my problems and solutions through with someone else.

We're all in this together; embrace the challenge!

—Luke Haravitch

MAJ, US Army

Dear friend and brother in arms

PREFACE

More Life

I know that life isn't always rainbows and unicorns. We are confronted daily with challenges of heartbreak, illness, and death. We can feel crushed under the weight of suffering and lose sight of our true blessings and purpose.

I make no assumptions about the path of our individual journeys, because the possibilities in our phenomenal world are endless. However, I do feel confident about our final destination. If I've learned nothing else from my personal story, it is that *life is a precious gift and we all must die.* Had my story ended on that tragic day at Range 47 when an explosion left me fighting for my life, I'd have nothing more to write. Fortunately, by God's grace, I awoke three days later in a hospital room surrounded by the comforting love of my family and friends.

In the days after the Fort Bragg training accident, I made a commitment—to myself and to God—to more wisely manage my time than I did during the years of my youth. I vowed to live each day with love and laughter. To serve my family, friends, and community with the gifts that God had given me. The scars on my face serve as a constant reminder of that commitment. When death comes for me (again), I want to know for certain my time was spent wisely. My time was spent purposefully.

Many inspirational mentors have shared their light over my path. Always guiding me to search within for what I don't understand without. They have encouraged me to listen to my heart, discipline my actions, and seek love and understanding in all I do. The famous Austrian psychiatrist and Holocaust survivor Viktor Frankl said, "We don't invent our mission; we detect it." We don't create our purpose; we find it! The pathfinder searches the road ahead to explore the possibilities. He bears a torch to light the way, not only for himself, but also for those that follow. May this book serve as my very own torch, a continuation to life after the fire, and my personal testimony to God's great gift of more life!

"In a thousand ways, he [Jesus] was saying that God comes to you disguised as your life!"
—Richard Rohr, *Things Hidden: Scripture as Spirituality*

INTRODUCTION

"Live and Love on Purpose"

> Jesus said unto him, Thou shalt love the Lord
> thy God with all thy heart, and with all thy
> soul, and with all thy mind. This is the first
> and great commandment. And the second
> is like unto it, Thou shalt love thy neighbour
> as thyself. On these two commandments
> hang all the law and the prophets.
> —MATTHEW 22:37–40 KJV

In my previous book, *Baptized by Fire*, I discussed my personal struggles after experiencing a life-changing accident during my time in the US Army. Out of the chaos of those years, a profound and adventurous relationship with God has emerged. It's been ten years since that painful day at Fort Bragg, and each morning still feels like Christmas. With each sunrise, I wake up and think to myself, *I can't believe I get another chance to make a difference in someone's life*. I get another chance to love my wife. I get another chance to grow with my children. Heck, I get another chance to live today better than I did yesterday. That's a pretty sweet deal! And it's all because of God's great gift called life.

Living on purpose is another way of saying living to reach your full potential. When we look around, we see that every living thing is working to grow. We are naturally programed to grow, heal, and recover. For example, think about the growth cycle of a lobster in the ocean. When the lobster has outgrown itself, it must shed the outer shell and lay vulnerable to prey for several days while it regrows a more spacious outer skeleton. Growth and regrowth are true for the lobster and for us! Good, bad, or indifferent, each experience in life draws us to a better version of ourselves.

If we look within ourselves with the right intentions, we can feel life pulling us along, urging us to grow through the challenges we face. We can recognize our potential and stop allowing the winds of change and challenge to blow us around. Pastor Rick Warren wrote in his book *The Purpose Driven Life*, "We are products of our past, but we don't have to be prisoners of it." God has a plan for us, and it's surely not to spend the rest of our days *taking punches on the chin*. We only need the courage to step out on this adventure in faith and trust in the love of God.

It's no secret that I made a spiritual course correction after getting hurt on that horrific day. The loss of my career, wound recovery, and personal trauma were just a bit too much for me to handle. I was lost and void of purpose. Everything I had known about myself was shattered in that explosion. Somehow, in all the hurt and pain, God sought me and found me broken and afraid. His grace has guided and protected me along this road of recovery. I've not been victimized or defeated one bit. God's love has mended parts of me that no surgery or therapy could ever heal.

Surprisingly, God's love isn't the only hero in the story. Countless caring people have shared their healing love with me. My wife, family, friends, doctors, nurses, coworkers, and mentors have all led me to understand the true power of love and community. My years after the accident have been the most fulfilling years of my life. Life is not just an endless cycle of suffering and loss. Life is a journey filled with endless opportunities to express God's love. Each day we can make a choice to share our gifts and talents with our family, friends, and community.

However, purposeful living is definitely not for the faint of heart. It's an ongoing relationship with God that opens our hearts to joy, peace, patience, kindness, goodness, faithfulness, gentleness, and self-control. It's a daily examination of your character and values. Living life on purpose is a commitment to share God's love in all you do. The healing power of love shared in my recovery is the very love I hope to share in the pages ahead.

"If God can give life to a dead man, he can give life to a dead career. He can bring life to that dead marriage. He can bring life to that dead dream. He can bring life to that financial dead end."
—Rick Warren

Dear friend,

This book explores four personal commitments to living a life of purpose and adventure. I believe these commitments are essential in overcoming challenges and reaching your full potential in life. In my years as an army soldier and now as a family therapist, I've learned natural principles never change and challenges never stop. These commitments will help you see challenges from a totally different perspective while each day pushing you to reflect on God's love and confronting the road ahead with confidence.

COMMITMENT #1

"Embrace the Challenge of Life"

> *Dear brothers and sisters, when troubles*
> *of any kind come your way, consider it an*
> *opportunity for great joy. For you know that*
> *when your faith is tested, your endurance*
> *has a chance to grow. So let it grow, for when*
> *your endurance is fully developed, you will*
> *be perfect and complete, needing nothing.*
> —JAMES 1:2–4 (NLT)

Embracing the challenges of life is the mind-set for living on purpose. None of us is exempt from life's challenges, and they show up in our lives every day, pushing and pulling us along a path of growth and healing. They follow us around like needy children in our interactions, habits, and beliefs, constantly urging and pleading to us for resolve. When left unattended, problems have a terrible reputation for finding their way into our worlds and wreaking havoc on the things we love the most. Our spiritual relationship, job, family, and physical health are the usual suspects to a ripe and juicy conflict. Just as gravity is always working as a natural law, helping us measure and make sense of the world around us, life's challenges are working to help us measure and make sense of ourselves! God is testing our faith and growing our endurance.

After the explosion, I was burned pretty badly, and working my way out of the hospital wasn't easy. I had to really psych myself up to get through a day of treatment and recovery. Sometimes I'd replay in my mind the rally speech my high-school football coach gave during halftime in an all-time rival game. Thinking back, his words reminded my teammates and me to take a closer look inside ourselves. If we really wanted to win, we had to get excited about the challenge the other team presented. He urged us to use the *energy of the challenge* as motivation to become a better version of ourselves. I'm thankful for that memory and the wisdom that lives on in my coach's words. If I wanted to pick up the pieces of my life, I needed to be prepared for the endless challenges that awaited me on the road to healing.

In those first tough weeks of recovery, each challenge I encountered was an opportunity to learn more about myself and God's will in my life. My personal health, marriage, family, and finances have all been frequent costumers of challenge. I've learned to embrace those challenges instead of ignoring them or falling victim to their power.

Problems aren't always easy to stomach, but they have a special kind of wisdom that is available in the suffering (*if we're listening*). Problems tell us things about ourselves that we often overlook. Maybe you're working too hard at your job and running the risk of burnout? Maybe you're not working hard enough and you need something to turn you on? Whatever the situations might be, you can be assured there is something to learn in the pain of problems.

However, finding God's wisdom in the suffering isn't particularly easy to do. When problems begin to pile up, we get anxious and soon overwhelmed. It's hard to reflect and control our emotions under stress, confusion, and pain. I believe these are God's tests of your spiritual and personal resolve. He has a way of reaching us during times of trial and struggle. Don't get swept away in the uncertainty and confusion that challenges can sometimes bring. Look to embrace the challenge with open arms. No matter how lost or trapped you might feel, the power of choice is a resource that can't be overlooked. We have the power to choose our response to any situation that life presents. When we exercise the power of choice through our decisions, we can influence the outcome. We can actually choose to apply empowering thoughts and actions to our difficult situations. Under the pressure of life's unique struggles, our power of choice is natural and always available. We should take advantage of it!

The Power of Choice

We tend not to think about death until it sneaks up behind us and taps us on the shoulder. The US Army gave me plenty of opportunities to think about death during my twelve-year military career. Like many other veterans, I've got a good bar story for every day of the week! Let's see; there is roadside-bomb Monday, mortar-attacks Tuesday, burning-building Wednesday, Man-Love Thursday, firefight Friday, suicide-bomber Saturday, and we can't forget Sunday brunch in the bunker. Ironically, death overlooked me during those dangerous experiences and found me during a random training accident at Fort Bragg, North Carolina. Like the ghost from Christmas past, I was ushered through an account of my life, reviewing the endless hours spent wasting time, chasing stupidity, and riding the wave of gratification. I felt remorse over the time and relationships I had mismanaged. I still can remember the sheer panic I felt as my power of choice faded with every drop of blood that left my body on that tragic day. I can recall that in my last moments of consciousness, I felt incomplete and powerless to change the future.

Several days later, I awoke to notice that death did not succeed. God had spared me during a time I thought was surely my last moments of life. After getting my wits about me in the hospital, I remember recognizing the predicament my mangled body was in. The bandages over my eyes concealed the long-term outcome of my vision. My leg was wrapped in a plastic vacuum and the burns and stitches were endless. The fears in my family and friends' faces were a close second to mine. Everyone was paralyzed in doubt and uncertainty about my future. As I pondered the future in fear, my power of choice was sneaking away once again. I was so caught up in my future prognosis and the challenges to come that I nearly missed the profound wisdom God had to offer in my circumstances. My power of choice! My power to choose my response to any situation life has to offer.

God's wisdom taught me that I could choose my response to my spiritual and physical limitations. I could use my situation to learn new ways to stretch beyond my comfort zone. I could focus my efforts on making healthy choices during unhealthy situations. The great teacher on leadership Dr. Stephen Covey said, "I am not a product of my circumstances. I am a product of my decisions."

Although I definitely needed help processing anger and making better decisions, I set my course on making better choices. I knew God's plan was not for me to remain a victim of misfortune and defeat any longer.

"The ultimate measure of a man is not where he stands in moments of comfort and convenience, but where he stands at times of challenge and controversy."
—Martin Luther King Jr.

Dear friend,

Having an embracing attitude toward life's trials has made all the difference in my self-worth and personal value. Every day we have to make a conscious effort to accept life's challenges as moments of personal and spiritual growth.

Embracing the challenge of life is a commitment to exercising your power of choice. Don't fall victim to the limitations and constraints that problems bring in your life. Life is the University of the Universe. Meet your challenge head on with the mind of a student and a spirit of curiosity.

Actions On

Below you will find inspiring scriptures to use for personal study, reflection, and meditation. Use the *Actions On* sections as the next steps to enhance your experience with this book. Take time out of your day to reflect, journal, and discuss your findings with others.

READ:

- *Trust in the LORD with all thine heart; and lean not unto thine own understanding.*

—Proverbs 3:5 KJV

PRAY:

- Father, my heart is open to the challenges and trials of the physical world. I look to you for guidance and wisdom so my faith and endurance can grow. Help me trust you and exercise my power of choice in the direction of purpose and love. Amen.

MEDITATE:

- *When thou passest through the waters, I will be with thee; and through the rivers, they shall not overflow thee: when thou walkest through the fire, thou shalt not be burned; neither shall the flame kindle upon thee.*

—Isaiah 43:2 KJV

Joe's Journal Points

"If you aren't in over your head, how do you know how tall you are?"
—T. S. Eliot

1. If you died today, would you be content? Why or why not?
2. Are you challenging yourself outside your comfort zone? How do you know?
3. What are the next steps to improve your attitude?
4. What challenges are you running from? Why?
5. What challenges are you embracing?
6. Rate your daily relationship with God on a scale from one to ten (poor to great).
7. What are the next steps to improve your spiritual relationship?

Notes

COMMITMENT #2

"I Am My Own Resource"

*Do your best to present yourself to
God as one approved, a worker who
does not need to be ashamed and who
correctly handles the word of truth.*
—Timothy 2:15 (NIV)

C an you recall the safety instructions flight attendants emphasize about wearing the oxygen mask? They always remind us to put our own mask on first before helping others. Have you ever wondered why a flight attendant would need to remind us about a task that seems so simple? Oddly enough, during an actual emergency, people tend to forget about themselves and look to others for safety and care. We either run to the rescue of others or wait helplessly for others to arrive. We often overlook our individual needs for survival or lie victimized in the face of extreme challenge.

Have you ever overlooked yourself hoping to serve someone else? Maybe you were so overextended you became more of the problem than a solution? Or you were in so much pain you gave up on yourself and everyone close to you? There's no way around it. Challenges have a way of pushing us to our breaking point!

I wish I could tell you a story about how extremely brave and stoic I was through my recovery. How I bounced back from the flames as a sentinel of war, ready to rejoin my comrades in arms! Unfortunately, that's not how the story played out at all. I lay victimized for a period of time in my recovery. The loss of my career, wound care, physical therapy, medications, and appointments were all too overwhelming. I did not run to the rescue of anyone nor did I tend to my own needs. I was a freakin' train wreck! I was in so much pain I gave up on myself and everyone close to me.

Ironically, I had enough of my wits to remain open to the whispers of God in those extreme periods of *suck*. I remembered how often God shows up in our suffering and leads us to learning. I began to listen. Let the story below be an example of how subtle blessings can find their way through subtle messengers.

Get in the Game

Every morning was the same routine. I would wake up, and the first thing on my agenda was to feel sorry for myself. Then I would take a handful of pills and rush to the couch to burry myself under a pile of blankets. Lying under the debris of shame, I would watch my wife and daughter leave to tackle the challenges of the day. I remained fixed on the couch in my self-pity and pain until they returned home from their daily adventures. This cycle happened every day like clockwork. Days turned into weeks and soon weeks into months.

Get up—feel sorry for myself, take pills, sleep, and repeat. Over and over again, I practiced this routine while my family struggled on.

Then one day, out of the blue, my young daughter Rhea rushed over to find me under the many layers of sadness and defeat. With great excitement, she rifled through the blankets, pulling layer after layer, to find her ungroomed, broken father hiding at the bottom. Gazing down on me with her big brown eyes, she asked a very simple question. "What are you going to do today, Daddy?" The questions seemed to fly from her mouth like an arrow heading straight for my soul. In hindsight, Rhea's question doesn't appear very profound. But in my attempts to offer a reply that morning, I had no words to return.

Like a ton of bricks, I lay there heavy and speechless as my wife and daughter ventured out to confront another day. Instantly, I reflected on my doctors, mentors, family, and friends who were all occupied diligently on my behalf. Everyone in my life was working so hard to make me whole. Everyone except me!

"What are you going to do today, Daddy?" Rhea's question lingered on. I had no reasonable answer for my child. I just couldn't see myself offering her the truth. I couldn't bring myself to say, "Well, sweetie, I intend to lay on the couch in my self-loathing and shame myself to sleep. I'll be right here when you return."

That moment changed my life! I realized that even under the pressure of extreme challenge, I was still capable of *doing* something about my circumstances. I realized the sun was intending to rise with or without me. The same twenty-four hours that were available before I got hurt were available to me now. Although I had new limitations that needed to be accepted, I was still an abled resource, and my daughter knew it. Rhea knew there was still plenty I could do to improve my position. If I wanted a different outcome to my pain and shame, she knew I had the power to choose my response to my present challenge.

From that day on, I made a commitment to be my own resource. Every problem, challenge, or struggle starts with me. I made a purposeful commitment to look inward at myself before I reach outward. I have the gift of choice in every situation, and I can choose to get in the game of life. My daughter Rhea's profound wisdom has never left my side. Her voice echoes loud and often these days.

Most folks are about as happy as they make up their minds to be.
—Abraham Lincoln

Dear Friend,

Remember, you are your own resource! Make small, positive choices and make them often. We might need lots of help and support from others, but the first resource is **you**!

Actions On

<u>READ:</u>

- *I can do all things through Christ which strengtheneth me.*
  —Philippians 4:13 KJV

<u>PRAY:</u>

- Father, give me the wisdom to look inward during periods of struggle. Help me see myself as the starting point to any situation. Guide me back into the game of life so I my improve my position with care to myself and love and service to others. Amen.

<u>MEDITATE:</u>

- Brethren, I count not myself to have apprehended: but this one thing I do, forgetting those things which are behind, and reaching forth unto those things which are before, I press toward the mark for the prize of the high calling of God in Christ Jesus.
  —Philippians 3:13–14 KJV

Joe's Journal Points

"Far better it to dare mighty things, to win glorious triumphs, even though checkered by failure, than to rank with those poor spirits who neither enjoy much nor suffer much, because they live in the gray twilight that knows no victory or defeat."

—Theodore Roosevelt

1. Have you ever felt defeat? What did you do?
2. What is stopping you from moving forward?
3. Do you believe in yourself?
4. How would you rate your self-care on a scale of one to ten (poor to great)?
5. When have you let yourself down in the past? Can you forgive yourself now?
6. What relationships in your life are overtaxed?
7. Where has God given you strength to overcome?
8. What do you need to ask God for today?

Notes

COMMITMENT #3

"Think and Act Only on what Serves You Well"

> *Finally, brethren, whatsoever things are true,*
> *whatsoever things are honest, whatsoever*
> *things are just, whatsoever things are pure,*
> *whatsoever things are lovely, whatsoever things*
> *are of good report; if there be any virtue, and*
> *if there be any praise, think on these things.*
> —PHILIPPIANS 4:8 KJV

admit there's no easy way to escape the physical and mental discomforts that come with pain and struggle. But your thoughts and feelings are not the same experience. We are God's artisanship of *Body, Mind,* and *Spirit.* Each unique part plays a key role in how we connect with our internal and external experience.

It is helpful to think of feelings as an alarm system that measures the amount of suck we experience during any given challenge. They help us recognize our likes and dislikes. Feeling is the body's way to communicate. Our feelings help us make sense of the world around us.

However, thoughts are more like GPS coordinates that point us toward our desires, passions, wants, and needs. Thought is the mind's way of communicating. The thoughts we choose to accept will soon turn into the actions we express. If we choose to accept the negative thoughts, we are likely to act in a negative way. The cycle reinforces negative feelings and soon a change reaction occurs. Negative feelings become negative thoughts, and negative thoughts become mistakes that you wish you could take back!

Has this every happened to you? Have you ever let your feelings control your thinking? Too often the feeling of hopelessness quickly grows into the thought of "I am hopeless!" Or the feelings associated with failure snowball into "I'm a loser!" And before you know it, you're thinking and acting like your feeling! Our feelings can seriously alter the way we think and act! The more we allow our feelings to influence our thinking, the more we trap ourselves in this turbulent cycle.

Early in my recovery, I was trapped in the vicious cycle of *feeling-based thinking*. I let my feelings of defeat influence my thoughts and actions. My feelings were so intense they became my reality. Soon the outside world looked just as miserable as my inside world. I wasn't prepared for the many changes and transitions that seemed to confront me all at once. Being a US Army engineer was all I knew how to do. My injuries clearly made it difficult for me to continue living the life I knew so well.

My challenge was staring me in the face, and I was too caught up in my feelings to see it clearly. Thankfully, God placed the help of a few caring mentors to guide me along the way. I learned very quickly that feelings-based thinking is a dangerous disposition.

Two Tears in a Bucket

Several months had passed since my accident at Range 47. My days were filled with lots of medical appointments, therapy sessions, and wound care. In an effort to ease the burden of recovery, Uncle Sam had assigned me a recovery advocate to help me along the way. Every week we would meet to discuss my medical care and the road moving forward.

One insightful day, we met when I was feeling extra sorry for myself. My cornea transplant had failed, the heat from the sun was no longer my friend, and my limitations made me feel helpless. My advocate noticed my discomfort and questioned my irritability. I gladly responded with a barrage of gripes about how unfair and misfortunate my situation was. "I can't run, I can't sleep, I can't hear, and I can't read!" I complained. "What job is there for me?" My advocate carefully listened and waited patiently until the debris of *Can Nots* had settled.

"Mr. Brazzle, I'm aware of the many challenges you're up against, but you've only mentioned the things you can't do. Now what?" he calmly inquired. Now what, I thought to myself. I looked to object but found no answer to return. I offered a meaningless shrug of the shoulders and he continued.

"My job is to help you look at the possibilities ahead. You have real limitations to consider and many challenges to confront, but we need to discuss the many things you can do." His words struck a major cord with me. I had been so wrapped up in my own suffering I had lost sight of the many blessings that were occurring despite my situation. I had only focused on the limitations in my life. I was consumed by the physical and mental pain of my recovery.

After leaving his office that day, I knew my thinking needed a major overhaul. I had too many real problems to solve than to dwell on the *Can Nots*. The recovery advocate's challenge rang in the back of my head for days. Now What...Now What...Now What? I wasn't sure about what was next, but I knew thinking about my limitations was useless. I needed to think about those things that were helpful. I needed to think about the tons of family support and friends helping me through this rough time. I needed to remember those who have suffered much greater loss for the same cause. I needed to refocus my energies and efforts on activities that promoted growth and healing. These thoughts and actions could have been helpful during my appointment in the story above. I am forever grateful for being reminded that day about the power of thoughts and actions.

> "Stand guard at the door of your mind."
> —Jim Rohn

Dear Friends,

The thoughts we choose to feed ourselves shape the way we see and act in the world. When I made the commitment to change my thought patterns, I had much less knowledge about the impact of our mind than I have today. This wisdom was available way before I learned about positive affirmations, brain functions, and energy. Read the words of Roman Emperor Marcus Aurelius, "You have power over your mind—not outside events. Realize this, and you will find strength." Written sometime around AD 176, his great insight still has meaning today.

Through my work as a family therapist, I've gained a greater understanding around the power of thought and its great impact on our actions. Here's a hard concept to grasp in theory but easy to learn by experience.

"You are not just feelings and thoughts!"

We are something bigger than that. We are God's creation of body, mind, and spirit. Our feelings and thoughts are just a small part of who we really are. Use your power of choice and pick the thoughts and actions that serve you best!

Actions On

<u>READ:</u>

- *Do not conform to the pattern of this world, but be transformed by the renewing of your mind. Then you will be able to test and approve what God's will is—his good, pleasing and perfect will.*

  —Romans 12:2 NIV

<u>PRAY:</u>

- Father, help me protect my mind against my limiting thoughts of negativity and blame. Guide my focus toward the many blessings available in the present moment. Your love, grace, and mercy will always be available to me. May I think often of your will operating in my life. Amen

<u>MEDITATE:</u>

- *Let all bitterness, and wrath, and anger, and clamour, and evil speaking, be put away from you, with all malice: And be ye kind one to another, tenderhearted, forgiving one another, even as God for Christ's sake hath forgiven you.*

  —Ephesians 4:31–32 KJV

Joe's Journal Points

> *"My actions are my only true belongings."*
> —Thick Nhat Hanh

1. How are your feelings controlling you?
2. What does an emotional outburst look like for you?
3. What are those unhelpful thoughts that keep coming back?
4. Rate how well you control your emotions on a scale from one to ten (poor to great).
5. How do you manage your stress?
6. What are you reading and watching every day? Is it helpful?
7. Write out ten truthful statements about yourself. Focus on the helpful ones!

Notes

COMMITMENT #4

"If I Say Yes, the Possibilities Are Endless"

> But Jesus looked at them and said to
> them, "With men this is impossible, but
> with God all things are possible."
> —MATHEW 19:26 NKJV

If you have made it this far in the book, you've probably noticed that all these commitments are about personal change. A change in the way we think, feel, and act around life's challenges. We began our story with embracing our challenges and confronting our experiences with an open heart. Then we discussed how all change starts with ourselves as the first and most valuable resource. We continued with identifying those never-ending thought patterns and the power to choose the thoughts that best serve us in the present moment. Now we are ready to listen within and find God's will pointing the way forward and urging us to try.

In commitment #3, we discussed how negative feelings are affecting the present moment we live in. Feelings such as fear, shame, and guilt cloud our judgments, vision, and understandings. You might recall a time when you were publicly embarrassed. Or a time when you were let down by a close friend or family member. Even worse, it might be a time you were physically injured or assaulted. What do you remember about those moments? Are you excited about doing those things again? Of course not! Those experiences can keep us from saying yes to the next opportunity.

Too often, we lie paralyzed in the grips of our own indecisiveness. Our fear of failure, hurt, and loss gets in the way of our willingness to try in the present. And before you know it, the weeks have turned into months and the months into years. Soon you realize you've let fear rule your life. You've let the failures of your past speak for the present moment and the future promise.

Saying Yes is an intentional act of faith that God will provide new opportunities for you to grow and change. Remember, God is always testing our faith and endurance. Saying Yes is also placing your trust in God and not in yourself or someone else.

Saying Yes in the face of challenges is the same as saying Yes to the many opportunities God has planned. Out of all the endless possibilities in the world, Yes is your ticket to participate in them. Yes is your admission ticket to show up to the game.

The great visionary Mahatma Gandhi said, "Be the change you wish to see in the world." I believe we must play a proactive role in shaping the world around us. Saying Yes is our way of confronting the day. Each day is another chance to show up ready to work and serve at the next opportunity God presents.

Dad's Wisdom

My father was never short of words on the topic of manhood and offered me this advice on the day I joined the US Army: "Volunteer for everything, son!" I pondered over his words that day but excused them as generic motivational dad talk. I wasn't' much for listening to the endless list of advice my dad had to offer. To make matters worse, I was a stubborn kid that had the whole world figured out. But somehow, I found his advice playing over and over in my head during the first few days of my army basic training.

Man, those days in basic were tough! It was definitely a big culture shock for a seventeen-year-old kid from Coatesville, Pennsylvania. It was a lot to process all at once, being in a new environment with tons of new people and crazy drill sergeants running around screaming at everybody that had moved the wrong way. Even in all the chaos, I remembered my dad's advice. "Volunteer for everything!" The meaning of his words became so obvious in the face of struggle. Say Yes to the moment! My dad was encouraging me to volunteer my service and value to others in return for opportunity.

As time went on, I came to deeply value my father's advice. I volunteered for every detail the army had to offer. Kitchen duty, cleaning detail, guard duty, ammo guard, fire watch, supply runner, cadence caller, and even leadership positions. Some of these jobs were the dumps! But I very quickly learned what my dad was trying to say. Volunteer for opportunities, son! Opportunities bring change, growth, learning, and adventure.

Working on detail in the army kitchen brought opportunities to eat earlier than I did before. I also had more food options available to choose from (although my drill sergeants weren't aware). Guard duty provided the opportunity for extra study time to prepare for the next day's test. That subtle blessing kept me sharp for Uncle Sam's high-stress atmosphere. Most importantly, I had endless opportunities to meet some really cool people. I had the chance to learn about their unique stories during all those volunteered assignments.

Where did they live? What family did they have? Why did they chose to join the army? I picked up all kinds of interesting bits about my battle buddies. My dad's advice led me to try new things. Saying Yes opened up a new world of learning and adventure for me. If you don't volunteer for life, you'll miss the opportunities.

> "Don't cry because it's over, smile because it happened."
> —Dr. Seuss

Dear Friends,

There is a power operating inside us beyond my best attempt of comprehension. I've discovered an internal driving force that pulls us along this adventure called life. It's more profound than our body or mind. It's a force pulling from the depths of our heart. If we listen deep inside ourselves, we can hear our spirit saying Yes to the next opportunity. The heart serves as your spiritual compass, always correcting our walk and pointing us toward God's love and wisdom. When you say Yes to life, you are saying Yes to the next opportunity. More importantly, you are saying Yes to God. Our journeys may look very different along the way, but at the very core of each person, the heart points toward adventure and growth.

Actions On
READ:

- When He had finished speaking, He said to Simon, "Push out into the deep water. Let down your nets for some fish." Simon said to Him, "Teacher, we have worked all night and we have caught nothing. But because You told me to, I will let the net down." When they had done this, they caught so many fish, their net started to break.

    —Luke 5: 4–6 NKJV

PRAY:

- Father, help me hear your voice in my heart. Allow my ears to ring with a never-ending Yes! May I see your will in every opportunity that I am presented, and when the road is tough, may I know you are close by. May I trust your guiding hand is helping me along the way. Amen.

MEDITATE:

- *What shall we then say to these things? If God be for us, who can be against us?*

    —Romans 8:31 KJV

Joe's Journal Points

"I find that the harder I work, the more luck I seem to have."
—Thomas Jefferson

1. What's stopping you from saying Yes?
2. Can you let God lead the way forward?
3. How has saying No robbed you of opportunity?
4. How much have you been trusting God on a scale from one to ten (least to most)?
5. When was the last time you volunteered?
6. How do you like to serve others?
7. What do you need to say Yes to today?

Notes

TOOLS & TIPS

"Grow with God"

Ask, and it shall be given you; seek, and ye shall
find; knock, and it shall be opened unto you.
—Matthew 7:7 KJV

As a marriage and family therapist, I work with relationships every day. I've seen relationships grow to unexpected heights of joy and satisfaction when both parties are intentional with their time and effort. When John spends more time and effort directed toward Sue, their relationship tends to grow! When Sue returns time and effort toward John, their relationship grows even more! Seems simple, right?

We are all drawn to learn about each other in relationships to gain deeper trust. The more trust we build in a relationship, the more love can grow. Loving God is no different. Investing your time and effort in God will build your trust in him.

"When you face things that are out of your control, you need something more than a positive mental attitude. You need faith in God, because he can control it when you can't. Most of life is beyond your control, so you need faith far more than you need positive thinking."

—Pastor Rick Warren

Jesus communed daily with God to seek guidance, counsel, and comfort. Jesus used scripture to confront evil and prayer to communicate and seek understanding from God. His interactions with the Almighty influenced his character, decisions, and interactions with others. Through these actions of reading and praying, Jesus understood love and the power it can have on others. Jesus's example is reminding us that God is our first and most important resource.

The opportunity to deeply connect with our Self, God, and others can only be found in our present experiences. Mindfulness is the vehicle for this deeper connection between present moment and experience. With practice, the quality of mindfulness aids clarity, self-awareness, and attention. Fr. Richard Rhor says mindfulness, or as he calls it, contemplation, is a "full-access knowing." In his book the *Naked Now*, he suggests that contemplation opens the heart and mind long enough to receive God's direction and grace.

Like Jesus, we should read, pray, and meditate to deepen our relationship with God. Seeking spiritual guidance helps set our compass heading and directs us on this crazy adventure. No journey is without its challenges and no challenges can be overcome without wisdom. Reading, prayer, and meditation are the tools needed to understand God's timeless wisdom for the road ahead no matter what crossroad or challenge you face.

Read Daily

Reading scriptures, inspirational, or devotional material is a great way to learn about God's wisdom throughout time. There are tons of books, eBooks, videos, or podcasts available for us to deepen our understanding of God. The important part is to be consistent with your study and make learning a life commitment. Below are a few good books worth the time to read.

1. The Holy Bible, King James Version
2. *Mere Christianity* by C. S. Lewis
3. *The Purpose Driven Life: What on Earth Am I Here For?* by Rick Warren
4. *Man's Search for Meaning* by Viktor E. Frankl
5. *The Miracle of Mindfulness* by Thich Nhat Hanh
6. *Living Buddha, Living Christ* by Thich Nhat Hanh
7. *The Naked Now* by Richard Rohr
8. *The Alchemist* by Paulo Coelho

Pray Daily

In Luke's Gospel, Jesus addresses his disciples' question on prayer. He sets an example of prayer for his disciples to follow. This is a great reference to ground yourself in prayer.

And it came to pass, that, as he was praying in a certain place, when he ceased, one of his disciples said unto him, Lord, teach us to pray, as John also taught his disciples. And he said unto them, When ye pray, say, Our Father which art in heaven, Hallowed be thy name. Thy kingdom come. Thy will be done, as in heaven, so in earth.

Give us day by day our daily bread.
And forgive us our sins; for we also forgive every one that is
indebted to us.
And lead us not into temptation; but deliver us from evil.
                                                    —Luke 11:1–4 KJV

Here are three additional prayers that you might find helpful during your daily travels.

Gratitude Prayer: Simply begin to list all the things that you are grateful for. Think about the small blessings God had placed in your life. Things such as health, food, shelter, family, friends, or even the weather. Continue this process until you have completely run out of mental energy. This mental purging is a great way to appreciate all the gifts God allows in our life.

Forgiveness Prayer: Begin with an honest confession of your shortcomings. This might be thoughts, emotions, attitudes, or actions that don't repersent the best parts of you. Continue this confession until your mind and heart are empty. Ask God for forgiveness in these areas and the strength to confront these flaws when they next appear. Character refinement is a lifelong process, and we start and end that journey with God's forgiveness.

Intentional Prayer: These are the prayers of our wants, needs, and hopes. We must be specific about the five W's—*who, what, when, where, and the how*—of the want.

If you want a financial increase or a better job, then first determine how much or what specific new job you want. If your intention is healing, be specific as to who and what should be healed. These prayers are the driving force of writing our future. Only when we are sure of what we want can God allow the universe to realign to our needs.

Meditate

Pastor Rick Warren cautions us, "Don't miss the ordinary moments; because in them we can do extraordinary things." So how can we stay mindful in this crazy thing called life? Daily meditation and self-care are the tools that keep us grounded to our passing experiences.

Often times, we find ourselves overwhelmed by the noise in our heads and the conflicts in our bodies. Just a few minutes of focused peace can help you reconnect to the presence of God and refocus on the purpose ahead. Meditation is a simple but essential skill you can use to calm the body and improve self-awareness.

Self-Guided Body Scan: Find a quiet place where you can settle and relax. Ground yourself with a chair or cushion or sit directly on the ground. Use a firm sitting posture, but don't be tense. Begin to focus your attention on each individual breath that you take. Notice how the air flows into your nose, down into your lungs, and deep into your core. Try to avoid high chest breathing. This is when you only allow the air to flow into the chest but not deep into your diaphragm or core. Deep breaths that flow through the core allow for the body's nervous system to relax. You can begin to guide your awareness to other parts of the body once you can easily inhale for four seconds and exhale for six seconds. Start by focusing on the top of the body at the head. Notice any signs of tightness, tension, or tingling. When any sign of the three *T's* appear, start to visualize clean air coming through your body and releasing the negative feelings. Continue to move down the body, noticing each connecting part. Spend as little or as much time as you need on each area of the body. Bring closure to your body scan with an awareness of gratitude—a true and honest recognition of the mind and body that serves you each day.

Set Positive Intentions: Setting positive intentions in our mind is critical to our mental health. With enough frequeny, our thoughts become our actions and our actions becomes our habits. We could say further, our habits become our character. In *The 7 Habits of Highly Effective People*, Steven Covey encourages effective people to visualize every detail of their desired outcome before acting on the physical work. Set positive outcomes for yourself and others. Write down key words or qoutes that inspire you to feel motivated and complete. Affirm your intentions in the postive and often!

Questions to Reflect Upon

What might I Keep Doing, Start Doing, and Stop Doing that will help me make strong commitments to myself so I may be able to move forward for greater well being and seeking peace?

Keep Doing: _____

Start Doing: _____

Stop Doing: _____

Grow Through Personal Values and Integrity

Personal values are the waypoints that guide our path and define our character. Eric Greitens, a retired Navy SEAL and *New York Times* best-selling author, said, "Arrogance is the armor worn by hollow men..." I had plenty of arrogance to pass around in the early years of my military career. Over time, Uncle Sam instilled the values in me needed to serve this great nation and more deeply define my character. My character benefited immensely from the army's value-based leadership and helped me identify several values that are foundational for me.

These are the values I find most helpful in my personal and professional life. What values have deep meaning for you? What values do you expect from others?

Courage: *For God has not given us a spirit of fear, but of power and of love and of a sound mind.*
—2 Timothy 1:7 NKJV

Love: *Jesus said unto him, Thou shalt love the Lord thy God with all thy heart, and with all thy soul, and with all thy mind. This is the first and great commandment.*

—Matthew 22:37–38 KJV

Adventure: *And he saith unto them, Follow me, and I will make you fishers of men.*

—Matthew 4:19

Service: *As every man hath received the gift, even so minister the same one to another, as good stewards of the manifold grace of God.*

—1 Peter 4:10 KJV

Spirituality: *Do not think that I have come to abolish the Law or the Prophets: I have not come to abolish them but to fulfill them.*

—Matthew 5:17 NIV

Staying honest with our values and ourselves is a never-ending process. Using God's word is a great way to reflect on your truth and refocus your values. Integrity is the action of staying true to those values. The pastor of Cliffdale Community Church, Morris Barnett, has a favorite saying: "God is more concerned about your character than your comfort!" One Sunday, he delivered a great message on developing your integrity and offered some practical wisdom. Pastor Morris Barnett preached, "To develop a character of integrity, you must ask for God's help to build these seven qualities..."

1. Pray for Understanding

Teach me, O Lord, the way of thy statutes; and I shall keep it unto the end. Give me understanding, and I shall keep thy law; yea, I shall observe it with my whole heart.

—Psalms 119:33–34 KJV

2. Pray for Consistency

Make me to go in the path of thy commandments; for therein do I delight.

—Psalms 119:35 KJV

3. Pray for Contentment

Incline my heart unto thy testimonies, and not to covetousness.

—Psalms 119:36 KJV

4. Pray for Discernment

Turn away mine eyes from beholding vanity; and quicken thou me in thy way.

—Psalms 119:37 KJV

5. Pray For Reassurance

Stablish thy word unto thy servant, who is devoted to thy fear.

—Psalms 119:38 KJV

6.   Pray for Victory

Turn away my reproach which I fear: for thy judgments are good.

—Psalms 119:39 KJV

7.   Pray for Endurance

Behold, I have longed after thy precepts: quicken me in thy righteousness.

—Psalms 119:40 (KJV)

Commit to Setting Goals

Murphy's Law is the age-old principle that states, *anything that can go wrong will go wrong.* That especially applies to those who make a focused effort to create personal change in their life.

Murphy's Law states

1.   If anything just cannot go wrong, it will anyway.
2.   Left to themselves, things tend to go from bad to worse.
3.   If you throw anything away, you will need it as soon as it is no longer available.
4.   Everything takes longer than you think.
5.   If it looks easy to repair, it's tough.
6.   If it looks tough, it's damn near impossible.
7.   You can't tell how deep a puddle is until you step in it.
8.   There are two lessons in life: painful and expensive.
9.   Nothing is as easy as it looks.
10. Every solution breeds new problems.

Setting a direction and committing to goals are priceless resources to prepare us for the unfortunate reality of Murphy's Law. How we think, speak, and act around Murphy's challenges can determine what comes next in our adventurous story.

Have you set personal goals for yourself? What direction are your goals taking you? Take a moment to reflect on the G.R.O.W. reflections below.

G.R.O.W.

Goal: Am I ready to set a goal that I am committed to working on, is within my circle of influence, and believe I can achieve?

Reality: I believe this goal is real for me to be able to achieve because:

Options: What options are available to me to work with others and myself as I start to work on my goal? List the options you have below.

Will: What will I specifically do to achieve my goal? List what you will do below.

Additional Readings

1. *Tao Te Ching*, by Lao Tzu, Chapter 63

> Practice non-action.
> Work without doing.
> Taste the tasteless.
> Magnify the small, increase the few.
> Reward the bitterness with care.
>
> See simplicity in the complicated.
> Achieve greatness in little things.
>
> In the universe the difficult things are done as if they are easy.
> In the universe great acts are made up of small deeds.
> The sage does not attempt anything very big,
> And thus achieves greatness.
>
> Easy promises make for little trust.
> Taking things lightly results in great difficulty.
> Because the sage always confronts difficulties,
> He never experiences them.

2. *Heading Home*

"Like all of us, the soldier walks the path of his life and finds himself under God's watchful eye, alone. He is bathed in a golden light that can only be called 'heavenly.' Like all God's children, his ultimate destination is a heavenly home, where he can know the sweet peace of divine love."

—Thomas Kinkade

3. *The Last Bridge*

"I believe that no man can be completely able to summon all his strength, all his will, all his energy, for the last desperate move, till he is convinced the last bridge is down behind him and there is nowhere to go but on.

—Heinrich Harrer

4. *Celebrate What Is Constant*

"It seems to me that one ought to rejoice in the fact of death—ought to decide, indeed, to earn one's death by confronting with passion the conundrum of life. One is responsible to life: It is the small beacon in that terrifying darkness from which we come and to which we shall return. One must negotiate this passage as nobly as possible...It is the responsibility of free men to trust and to celebrate what is constant—birth, struggle, and death are constant, and so is love, though we may not always think so—and to apprehend the nature of change, to be able and willing to change. I speak of change not on the surface but in the depths—change in the sense of renewal.

But renewal becomes impossible if one supposes things to be constant that are not—safety, for example, or money, or power. One clings then to chimeras, by which one can only be betrayed, and the entire hope—the entire possibility of freedom disappears."

—James Baldwin

5. *To Laugh Is to Risk*

To laugh is to risk appearing a fool,
To weep is to risk appearing sentimental.
To reach out to another is to risk involvement,
To expose feelings is to risk exposing your true self.
To place your ideas and dreams before a crowd is to risk their loss.
To love is to risk not being loved in return,
To live is to risk dying,
To hope is to risk despair,
To try is to risk failure.
But risks must be taken because the greatest hazard in life is to risk nothing.
The person who risks nothing, does nothing, has nothing, is nothing.

—"To Risk" by William Arthur Ward

6. *The Wise Man...Being Last & Unselfish*

The sky is everlasting
And the earth is very old.
Why so? Because the world
Exists not for itself;

It can and will live on.
The Wise Man chooses to be last
And so becomes the first of all;
Denying self, he too is saved.
For does he not fulfillment find
In being an unselfish man?

—Lao Tzu, *Tao Te Ching*

7. *Leadership*

If you want to inspire devotion, be devoted.
If you want to inspire belief, believe.
If you want to motivate, be motivated.

—Eric Greitens, *Resilience: Hard Won Wisdom for
Living a Better Life*

8. *We Do Not Believe in Ourselves*

"We do not believe in ourselves until someone reveals that deep inside us something is valuable, worth listening to, worthy of our trust, sacred to our touch. Once we believe in ourselves we can risk curiosity, wonder, spontaneous delight or any experience that reveals the human spirit."

—E. E. Cummings

9. *Future Worry*

"Never let the future disturb you. You will meet it, if you have to, with the same weapons of reason which today arm you against the present."

—Marcus Aurelius

10. *Healing in Your Wounds*

"Other people are going to find healing in your wounds. Your greatest life messages and your most effective ministry will come out of your deepest hurts."

—Rick Warren

11. *Sow a Thought*

"Sow a thought, reap an action; sow an action, reap a habit; sow a habit, reap a character; sow a character, reap a destiny."

—Stephen Covey

12. *We Are Travelers*

"We are travelers on a cosmic journey, stardust, swirling and dancing in the eddies and whirlpools of infinity. Life is eternal. We have stopped for a moment to encounter each other, to meet, to love, to share. This is a precious moment. It is a little parenthesis in eternity."

—Paulo Coelho

BIBLIOGRAPHY

Aurelius, M., & G. Long. *Meditations*. Mineola, NY: Dover Publications, 1997.

Covey, S. R. *The 7 Habits of Highly Effective People: Powerful Lessons in Personal Change*. New York: Simon & Schuster, 2013.

Frankl, V. E. *Man's Search for Meaning*. Boston: Beacon Press, 2006.

Gandhi, M. *An Autobiography, or, The Story of My Experiments with Truth*. Lexington, KY: Renaissance Classics, 2012.

Greitens, E. *Resilience: Hard Won Wisdom for Living a Better Life*. Boston: Mariner Books/Houghton Mifflin Harcourt, 2016.

Rohr, R. *Things Hidden: Scripture as Spirituality*. Cincinnati, OH: Franciscan Media, 2008.

Warren, R. *The Purpose Driven Life: What on Earth Am I Here For?* Grand Rapids, MI: Zondervan, 2002.